PAISLEY
THE PILOT

I0179282

AND THE SKY HIGH DAY
BY SHEREE UTASH, ED.D AND MANDY FOUSE

PAISLEY
THE PILOT
AND THE SKY HIGH DAY

Copyright© 2025.
Wichita State University Campus of Applied Sciences and Technology (WSU Tech)
All Rights Reserved.

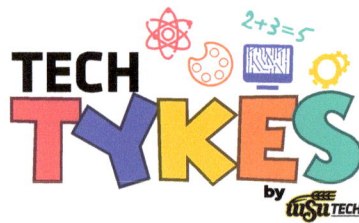

TECH TYKES by WSU TECH

SPARKING CURIOSITY IN SCIENCE,
TECHNOLOGY, ENGINEERING,
ART, AND MATH

Illustrated by Jesús Gallardo

ISBN: 978-1961600-09-6

FIG FACTOR MEDIA

WSU TECH

2

To the people of Wichita, the Air Capital of the World, who prove time and time again that when a community comes together, anything is possible. This city is built by dreamers, makers, and doers, and it continues to soar because of the relentless spirit of those who call it home.

To the workforce that fuels our skies and the educators who shape the next generation, your dedication ensures that innovation never stops. And to the future aviators, engineers, and explorers, may your curiosity lead you to great heights. The sky's the limit!

And to Grayson, Ella, Noah, Bryson, Eevy, Porter, Paisley, Emry, Beckham, and Parker, thank you for inspiring the characters that bring these stories to life.

Hi, I'm Paisley! I live in the Air Capital of the World, where lots of airplanes are made and zoom across the sky every day. They're fast, loud, and so cool! I have a group of friends. We call ourselves the Tech Tykes, and we dream about what we'll be when we grow up. We love going on adventures, using our imaginations, and solving problems!

I may only be six, but my eyes are always on the sky. At the playground, I love climbing to the top of the jungle gym, pretending I'm a pilot, and flying my friends (the Tech Tykes) across the sky.

Do you know what a pilot is?
A pilot is a person who flies airplanes high in the sky, carrying people and packages to faraway places. Pilots are brave, smart, and adventurous—just like me!

One summer, I went to an airshow, and a pilot let me sit in their plane! Since then, I've loved airplanes and anything that can fly. For my birthday, I asked for pilot stuff. I got a flight suit, a purple jacket, a hat, and goggles. Now I wear them everywhere, even to school!

My *Abuela* (that's my grandma) and *Abuelo* (that's my grandpa) always tell me, "You can do anything you set your mind to, *Mija* (that's what they call me)." And they're right!

Paper
Airplane
Contest
at the Aviation Museum
win a flight in a
B29 SUPERFORTRESS

One day after school, I saw a big poster on the wall. It had blue letters and a picture of an airplane.

It said, "Paper Airplane Contest at the Aviation Museum. Win a Flight in a B29 SUPERFORTRESS!"

My eyes got big. A ride in a big plane like a Superfortress? That would be a dream come true!

That's when I heard laughing behind me.

"You're too little to win!" a boy said.

"And girls can't be pilots," another boy added, pointing at my flight suit.

My cheeks got hot. I wanted to yell, "Yes, we can!" But instead, I ran home.

When I got there, I told *Abuela* and *Abuelo* about the contest (and the mean boys).

Abuela gave me a hug. "You can do anything, *Mija*," she said.

"You are brave and smart, just like a pilot," Abuelo said with a wink.

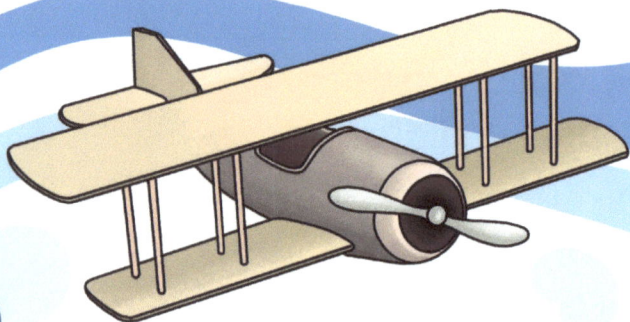

The next weekend, we went to the aviation museum for the big contest.

"Whoa!" I said when I saw the airplanes sparkling in the sun. Some were silver, and others had colorful stripes and designs. My favorite was the giant, shiny B29 Superfortress. "Look at those wings!" I said." "They're so big!"

"Pilots who fly these need steady hands and brave hearts," *Abuelo* said as we walked inside.

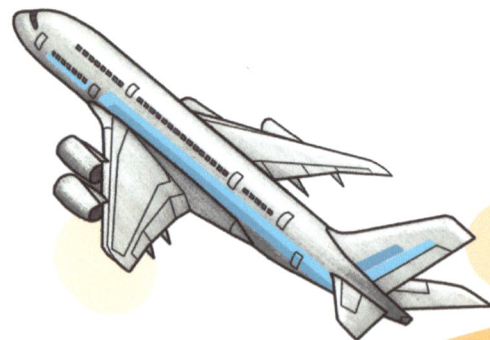

As we headed into the museum, I thought about how pilots watch the sky, make fast choices, and stay calm no matter what.

Like a pilot, I had to be ready and careful.

The room was full of kids testing their paper airplanes. Some of the older kids had planes with fancy wings and bright colors. I held my plane tight, got in line, and waited my turn.

Paper Airplane Contest

at the Aviation Museum
win a flight in a
B29 SUPERFORTRESS

That's when I saw them. It was the boys who had teased me at school. They laughed and pointed at other kids' planes, and I hoped they wouldn't see me.

"Good luck. You're going to need it!" one of them said from across the room, tossing his red paper airplane. My cheeks felt hot again, but I whispered, "I can do this," and fixed my airplane to make sure it flew straight.

A boy with messy brown hair and glasses got in line behind me. "Don't let them bug you," he said, looking at the boys who teased me. "Pilots have brave hearts and steady hands. You've got this." I blinked in surprise.

"That's what my *Abuelo* says! My name is Paisley, and someday I want to be a pilot," I said, smiling at him. "I'm Grayson," he replied. "Your plane looks really cool." "Thanks," I said, feeling a little braver.

Grayson reminded me that I wasn't just here to win but to show myself that I could do anything if I tried.

Just then, the bell rang. The room got quiet, and the contest began. One by one, kids threw their paper airplanes. Some flew high, and some dropped fast. The judges marked each landing spot. Then, it was my turn. I held my airplane tight and took a deep breath.

"Go show them how a real pilot flies," Grayson whispered, giving me a thumbs-up. The judge counted, "3... 2... 1... GO!"

I threw my airplane as hard as I could. It zoomed through the air, soaring and gliding before landing past all the others. For a second, no one said a word. Then, the crowd cheered! I smiled big.

It was almost over when an older boy stepped up and threw his plane. It zoomed across the room, barely missing mine, and landed just inches away. The judge walked over and looked at both planes.

They looked serious as they carefully measured them. I held my breath and my hands tight together. Finally, the judge spoke.

"This was a close race today, but we have a winner!" The room got quiet. **"Winning a ride in the B29 Superfortress is...Paisley!"** The crowd cheered! I jumped up and down, my ponytails bouncing. And my new friend Grayson gave me a big high five!

WINNER

After what felt like forever, the big day arrived. It was time to fly. My heart pounded as I climbed up the ladder into the shiny silver B29 Superfortress. The pilot, wearing a clean uniform, smiled at me in my flight suit and purple bomber jacket. "Ready, Paisley?" he asked. **"Let's FLY!"** I said, putting on my headset. *Abuelo* sat near me, giving me a thumbs-up.

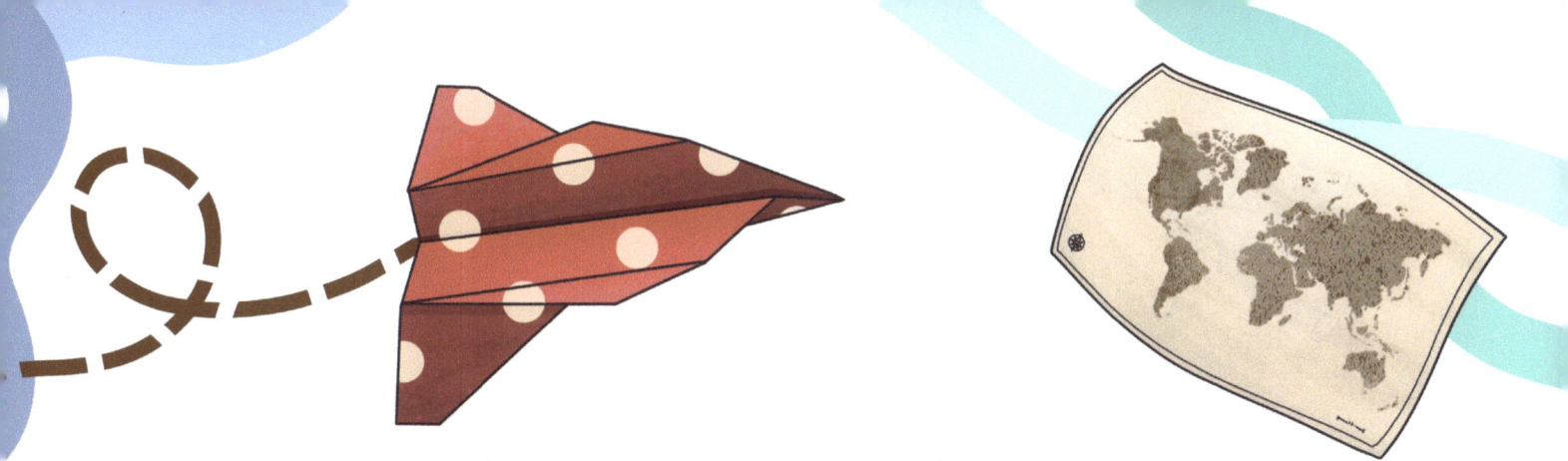

As the engines roared, the pilot said, "Did you know this plane was built with the help of women riveters during the war? They worked hard to make aviation history. " "Girls helped build this plane?" I asked. "Yes! They worked in factories, using tools to build these planes when there weren't enough men to do the job," the pilot said.

"And women fly planes too, just like I do."

"Do you think I can be a pilot when I grow up? " I asked nervously. "Of course," said the pilot, "A brave kid like you? The sky is the limit."

At that moment, I felt the wheels leave the ground. We were flying! The plane soared through the sky, and I pressed my nose to the window. The world below was so big, but everything seemed so small. It felt like being on the top of the jungle gym times a million!

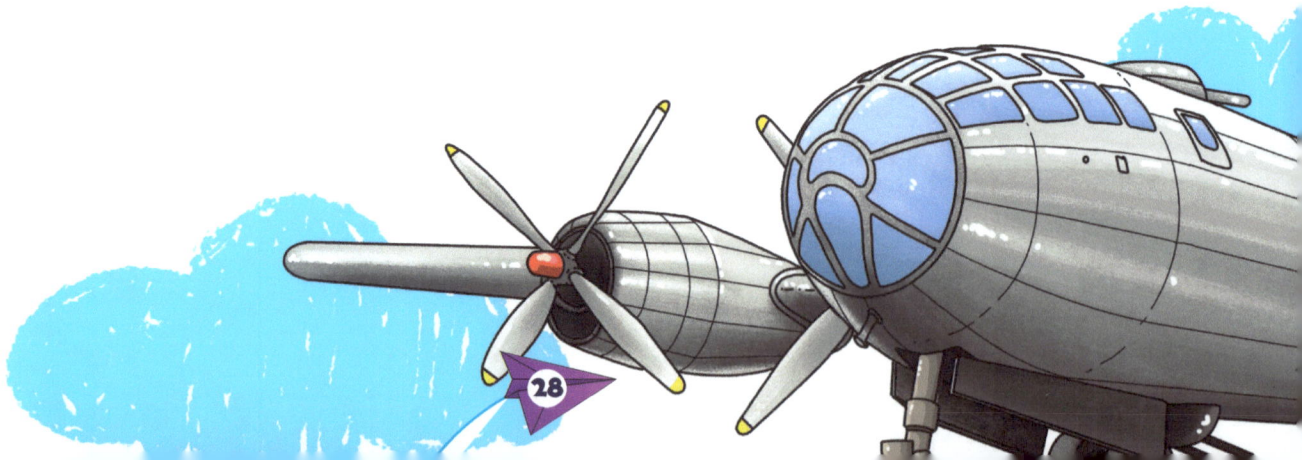

I looked over at the pilot. His hands rested on a big steering wheel, steady and sure. He watched the round dials in front of him, checking each one carefully. "This one tells me how high we're flying," he said, pointing to a dial with numbers that moved like a clock. "And this one helps me stay on the right path."

I watched as he gently turned the wheel, and the huge plane tilted just a little. "I have to make small changes all the time to keep us flying smoothly," he added with a smile.

I couldn't believe how many buttons, levers, and dials it took to fly such a big plane! "Pilots really do have steady hands and brave hearts," I thought.

When we landed, I couldn't stop smiling. Abuelo hugged me as I climbed down the steps, and *Abuela* proudly gave me a thumbs-up.

"You were born to fly, *Mija*," *Abuela* said.

"One day, I'll fly a plane just like this," I told her, looking back at the big shiny plane behind me.

That night, I sat on my bed, holding the little toy airplane the pilot gave me. I looked out the window at the moon and dark sky.

"Someday, I'll be a pilot and fly all the way to the stars," I whispered.

I thought about the contest, the women builders, and the ride in the big plane. I knew I could do anything if I tried my best because I'm Paisley, and the sky's the limit.

ABOUT THE AUTHORS

Dr. Sheree Utash, Ed.D., is a proud Wichitan, leader, and educator, but she's a mom, daughter, and a Gigi (grandma) first! As president of WSU Tech, she's dedicated to creating opportunities for students to achieve their dreams, but her favorite moments are spent cheering on her grandchildren and celebrating their curiosity and achievements. Sheree believes in the power of education to transform lives and communities—one learner at a time.

Mandy Fouse is a Wichita native, communications expert, and passionate mom to two young, imaginative minds. At WSU Tech, she leads efforts to craft and share stories that inspire and connect people, showcasing the incredible work being done across the college. Mandy believes that every student and individual has a story worth telling. She works to highlight the voices of tomorrow's leaders and inspire the next generation of thinkers and doers.

All proceeds from the Tech Tykes series will support WSU Tech's efforts to inspire and prepare the next generation of innovators, creators, and problem-solvers. Funds will be used to enhance educational opportunities, ensuring young learners have access to hands-on experiences that spark a lifelong love of science, technology, engineering, arts, and mathematics (STEAM).

www.ingramcontent.com/pod-product-compliance
Lightning Source LLC
Chambersburg PA
CBHW041431090426
42744CB00003B/36